To

_____

From

_____

Date

_____

Gentle Prayers *for* Hope *and* Healing

Photography by

Betty Fletcher

Hope Lyda, *General Editor*

HARVEST HOUSE PUBLISHERS
EUGENE, OREGON

May the God of hope fill you with all joy and peace as you trust in him,

so that you may overflow with hope by the power of the Holy Spirit.

ROMANS 15:13

Gentle Prayers *for* Hope *and* Healing

Text copyright © 2013 by Harvest House Publishers

-Photography copyright © 2013 by Betty Fletcher. Many of the photos used in this book were taken at Schreiner's Iris Gardens, Salem, Oregon. Used by permission.

Published by Harvest House Publishers • Eugene, Oregon 97402
www.harvesthousepublishers.com

ISBN 978-0-7369-4676-6

Design and production by Left Coast Design, Portland, Oregon

Special thanks to the women whose written prayers and selected verses shape the comforting heart of this book: Sharon Burke, Jean Christen, Betty Fletcher, Barb Gordon, Laura Knudson, Hope Lyda, Pat Mathis, Carolyn McCready, Becky Miller, Kim Moore, Sharon Shook, Georgia Varozza, LaRae Weikert, and Peggy Wright.

Printed in China

13 14 15 16 17 18 19 20 / LP / 10 9 8 7 6 5 4 3 2 1

Dear Friend,

$\mathcal{D}$id it happen to you? Did you have your life planned out and then all of a sudden find yourself on a path you never planned and on a journey you have no control over?

It happened to me. I found myself diagnosed with breast cancer, facing surgery and several months of chemotherapy and radiation treatments. During my cancer treatment, I had days when I was just too weary to pray. Oh, how I needed help from God and the prayers from others to get me through each day. This special prayer book, which originated in the hearts of prayerful women, was given to me to lead my heart to God's care when I just didn't have the strength to do so myself.

I don't know what you are facing today, but I do know that sometimes you get to a point where you can't or just don't know what to pray. May this book of special prayers stand in the gap and fill your heart with peace, comfort, strength, and especially the hope you need in this moment and for this journey.

Praying for you,

Mary Cooper

Gentle Prayers

Comfort

You are my hiding place;

you will protect me from trouble

and surround me with songs of deliverance.

PSALM 32:7

God, Your peace and comfort cover me as I walk this difficult journey. Your presence provides shelter from this storm. Your love soothes my anxious mind. And Your grace eases the burdens of my heart, body, and soul.

Are not two sparrows sold for a penny?
Yet not one of them will fall to the ground
outside your Father's care. And even the very
hairs of your head are all numbered. So don't be
afraid; you are worth more than many sparrows.

MATTHEW 10:29-31

*L*ord, give me faith that what You are doing in me and around me is all in Your control. Help me live in the moment with You. I know You care for the sparrows, and somehow You care for me even more. Thank You. Amen.

The LORD *replied, "My Presence will go with you, and I will give you rest."*

EXODUS 33:14

*A*s I travel this road and in my humanness question why, may I be mindful of Your promises to comfort, love, protect, uphold, and hear me. My mind and heart know that You are with me and that You're watching over me. Draw near to me now. Make Your presence strong enough that I may feel Your love.

Know that the LORD is God.

It is he who made us, and we are his;

we are his people, the sheep of his pasture.

PSALM 100:3

Father, what a comfort You are to me these days. When I'm down, You give me peace. When I'm up, You rejoice with me. No matter how I'm doing, I know I can turn to Your love and it will fill my body with warmth and my soul with hope. Thank You.

The LORD your God is with you,
the Mighty Warrior who saves.
He will take great delight in you.

ZEPHANIAH 3:17

Father, I ask You to surround
me today with Your comfort.
Help me feel the comfort of Your
presence and Your protective
strength. Lead me in the way of
peace, praise, and hope.

Rise up and help us;

rescue us because of your unfailing love.

PSALM 44:26

ℒord, on many days I want to turn away this unwelcome intruder in my life. I can easily give in to melancholy when I think about what I could do if only I were healthy. But then I remember that even these days come straight from Your holy hand. And though I was taken by surprise, You were not. That thought gives me such comfort!

I, even I, am he who comforts you...

who stretches out the heavens

and who lays the foundations of the earth...

For I am the LORD *your God.*

ISAIAH 51:12-13,15

𝒞reator, You shaped the stars and the heavens just as You shaped my heart, body, and soul. I search the sky for answers, and I see that Your light is already leading me from within.

Strength

I lift up my eyes to the mountains—
where does my help come from?
My help comes from the Lord,
the Maker of heaven and earth.

PSALM 121:1-2

Father, I need You to be my refuge today. Surround me with Your presence and peace so I may rest, knowing You have my life in Your hands. Give me hope as I face the future believing I can do all things through Christ. May Your joy be my strength, Lord.

Whom have I in heaven but you?

And earth has nothing I desire besides you.

My flesh and my heart may fail,

but God is the strength of my heart

and my portion forever.

PSALM 73:25-26

ather, I hurt.

I'm weak and tired.

Would You hold me?

Tighter please.

The LORD is my strength and song,

And He has become my salvation;

He is my God, and I will praise Him.

EXODUS 15:2 NKJV

hank You for the people who will be by my side as I go through this day. I know they are "Your hands" loving and caring for me. Give me strength, Lord Jesus, and carry me when I feel I cannot walk.

I rise before dawn and cry for help;
I have put my hope in your word.

PSALM 119:147

ord, I'm so glad Your Word is buried in my heart. It gives me strength when I need it most. At just the right moment, snippets of Your Word will burst across my memory: "Forget the former things and do not dwell on the past." Your mercies are new every morning, Lord. "I have loved you with an everlasting love and I have drawn you with loving-kindness. I will build you up again." I am precious in Your sight, Lord, and I know You love me and always have my best interests in Your heart.

He gives strength to the weary
and increases the power of the weak.
ISAIAH 40:29

Look to the LORD and his strength;
seek his face always.
Remember the wonders he has done,
his miracles, and the judgments he pronounced.
PSALM 105:4-5

*F*ather, thank You for being the strength of my heart and my portion forever. You are loving toward all You have made. I have known Your love in the past, I experience it in the present, and I am confident of it in the future.

*L*ord, please use me to bless others through my own struggle with this disease. Give me a prayerful heart for others. I want to be an instrument in Your hands. Thank You for hearing my prayer and being my source of strength.

May integrity and uprightness protect me,
because my hope, LORD, is in you.

PSALM 25:21

*ord, use this life to teach me,
strengthen me, and to anchor me
ever deeper in Christ Jesus. Teach me how
to soak up physical, emotional, and spiritual
moments and let them regenerate my spirit, my
body, and my mind. Let my joy and Your light be
that much more intense in the darkness. In Jesus'
name, amen.

Those who hope in the LORD
will renew their strength.
They will soar on wings like eagles;
they will run and not grow weary,
they will walk and not be faint.

ISAIAH 40:31

*ord, I look to You every moment. Please
sustain me when I grow weary, and
comfort my heart when I grow fearful. You are
unfathomably wise, and I trust You with this life
You have given me.

Healing

*Restore us, L*ORD *God Almighty;*
make your face shine on us,
that we may be saved.

PSALM 80:19

Lord, You knit me together in my mother's
womb,
Love in every stitch.
Now protect the work of Your hands.
Repair the threads of my life.
I trust You.

The LORD will fight for you; you need only to be still.

EXODUS 14:14

*D*ear Lord, I feel weak today. But I know that You are with me and that You are powerful, so I agree just to rest in Your hands. Help me to breathe in Your presence with every breath I take. I remember that You made me, so You know exactly how each part of my body works. I give You thanks for the work You are doing in me, though that work is sometimes difficult to see or feel. And I am grateful for Your tender care and provision exactly when I need it. Amen.

Gracious words are a honeycomb, sweet to the soul and healing to the bones.

PROVERBS 16:24

*G*od, I crave Your nourishment, refuge, and help. Even when I'm weary, I find myself wanting to be strong for others. Hold back my need to be their rock or their comforter even when I long to be those things. I know that only You can offer the strength they need, just as You are my only source. Thank You for being that loving presence for me and my loved ones. Amen.

My comfort in my suffering is this:
Your promise preserves my life.

PSALM 119:50

Father, I look to You for moments
to smile—even laugh—in this new and
unexpected experience. Lift my heart, my Lord.

May the LORD answer you when you are in distress;
may the name of the God of Jacob protect you.
May he send you help from the sanctuary.

PSALM 20:1-2

I would have lost heart, unless I had believed
that I would see the goodness of the LORD
in the land of the living.

PSALM 27:13 NKJV

Lord, this is not only a physical battle but also an emotional battle for me. Even though I've been told what to expect, I don't know how I will feel until I get there. Help me to deal with whatever comes my way today.

Father, I ask You to send me help from the sanctuary today. I cry out to You. I am weak and in need of Your protection and covering as I go through my day. Help me to see Your goodness and mercy. Help me to feel Your presence and the warmth of Your love. Great is Your name and greatly to be praised. I will look for and lean on Your help today, Lord.

Come to me, all you who are weary and burdened, and I will give you rest.

MATTHEW 11:28

*L*ord, tuck me under Your wings of healing, hide me in Your holy robes, and breathe health and wholeness and life and peace into me. Speak with Your powerful voice into my body and cause my cells to heal. Father, hold me in Your holy arms and find blessing in my love for You. I rest in Your holy hands. In Jesus' name, I pray. Amen.

I can do all this through him who gives me strength.

PHILIPPIANS 4:13

*G*od, when I first got the news of my trouble, I could not take it in. I'm still feeling overwhelmed, but You know that. In fact, there's nothing in my life that escapes Your loving notice. It's true that I might have lost heart, except for one all-important fact: You have promised to never leave me nor forsake me, and according to Your Word, that hope can never be cut off.

Peace

Return to your rest, my soul,
for the LORD has been good to you.

PSALM 116:7

Lord, I look to You when I come to the end of myself. Please hold my hand. Wrap me close to Your heart. Help me absorb Your warmth and strength and peace so I can go on. You are the source of life. You are the author of my life.

I sought the Lord, and he answered me;
he delivered me from all my fears.

PSALM 34:4

God, I pray for a quiet space to think over all that has happened and measure it against Your perfect will for me. May my thoughts and Your will become the same. I ask for courage and stamina to wade through this experience and face the facts. I need peace to hear the truth and consider it carefully. Please, Lord, I need Your holy healing from Your loving hands. I pray this in Jesus' name. Amen.

I will restore you to health
and heal your wounds.

JEREMIAH 30:17

My Comfort, give me the peace to release fear, guilt, anxiety, negativity, control, matters that drain my energy, and earthly priorities that conflict with Your heart. Most of all, I release my every need to Your care. This struggle is a part of my life—my being—right now. Today I turn it over to You with hope for transformation, just as I do every other part of my life.

Trust in the Lord with all your heart
and lean not on your own understanding.

PROVERBS 3:5

*L*ord, I will choose to trust You with all my heart, soul, and mind today. You have promised me, O Lord, to keep me in perfect peace as I set my mind on You.

A heart at peace gives life to the body.

PROVERBS 14:30

*L*ord, my heart and mind are restless, as are my body and spirit. In this moment all I can do is repeat over and over that You love me and that You want Your child to be whole. I am Yours and You are my Lord. How this sweet truth carries me to peace.

Hope

*The LORD is trustworthy in all he promises
and faithful in all he does.*

PSALM 145:13

Father, I pray that You inspire me with Your Word, with Your peace, and with a sense of Your purpose as I begin this day. You are the Lord God and Creator of everything. You are my creator and my Lord. You are the maker of my body and keeper of my future. I love You, Lord, and I love Your ways. I bow only before You today. In Jesus' name, I pray.

Take my yoke upon you and learn from me, for I am gentle and humble in heart, and you will find rest for your souls.

MATTHEW 11:29

*L*ord, help me release my worries so that I can hold on to Your hope. Don't let me dwell in the land of "what if" so I can live without fear in this moment of grace. For this day all I need is to stand in the light of Your love.

Good news gives health to the bones.

PROVERBS 15:30

*F*ather, You call me the apple of Your eye, and I know You cannot separate Yourself from my pain and sadness. Thank You for knowing me intimately. Thank You for being the one who stands over me constantly and who loves me completely. Lord, I ask You to take away the pain, the heartache, the fear, the suffering, the questions, and the burden of the unknown. I exchange these for Your peace. The good news of Your tender care renews my hope and strength.

Be joyful in hope, patient in affliction, faithful in prayer.

ROMANS 12:12

ℛ

Lord, I thank You for each new day. I thank You for my family and my friends. I thank You for their faithfulness to pray for me. It means so much. Give them hope and healing for this journey as well.

Hold on to what is good.

1 THESSALONIANS 5:21

ℛ

Throughout this season, Lord, You are the goodness and the grace. I reach out to You, and You reach out to me. On the hardest days when I am too tired to hold on to anything, You cradle me in Your arms and breathe hope back into my heart.

Gratitude

In this world you will have trouble. But take heart! I have overcome the world.

JOHN 16:33

Lord, [we] come to You with a heart of thanksgiving even though [we] may not understand everything that is happening right now. You are my [our] strength. [we] trust in You, and [we] cannot do this without You.

From birth I have relied on you;

*   you brought me forth from my mother's womb.*

I will ever praise you.

PSALM 71:6

ord, give me an opportunity to encourage
someone today. Even in this uncertain
time, let people see You in me. Help me show them
that You are the light they are looking for. I love
You, and I long for them to know You. What an
amazing privilege it is to participate in sharing the
good news of who You are.

[handwritten annotations: "us the" above "me an"; "tomorrow" above "today"; "us!" above "me"; "us" above; "we" near "I love"; "we" below]

[handwritten:] These and all things we pray! Amen

I will bring health and healing to it; I will heal
my people and will let them enjoy abundant
peace and security.

JEREMIAH 33:6

ord, I am so blessed that You see me as
Your beautiful child. You know my
thoughts and struggles in a way no one else can.
I am weak but You are strong! I am comforted
because I know You understand and are with
me to help me through this—all of this.

This day is holy to our Lord. Do not grieve, for the joy of the LORD is your strength.

NEHEMIAH 8:10

Lord, as I wake up this morning knowing that it will be a difficult day, I am afraid. I know in my heart You will walk with me through every minute of today. You are the light in the middle of my darkness, and I keep my eyes on You.

Create in me a pure heart, O God,

and renew a steadfast spirit within me.

PSALM 51:10

My sweet Jesus, thank You for being by my side each moment of my day and never leaving nor forsaking me. I recognize Your handiwork of love generously poured out from one hour to the next. Floods of joy and gratitude invade my heart when I see and experience Your blessings. Thank You that I have never been alone, and that I will never be alone.

Praise the LORD, my soul;

 all my inmost being, praise his holy name.

Praise the LORD, my soul,

 and forget not all his benefits—

who forgives all your sins

 and heals all your diseases,

who redeems your life from the pit

 and crowns you with love and compassion,

who satisfies your desires with good things

 so that your youth is renewed like the eagle's.

PSALM 103:1-5

Thank You for the good that is in my life. I witness and experience Your love through my family, my friends, the graceful trees, the rainbow of colors sprouting in the flower garden, and the whisper of You in all the beautiful miracles that surround me.

Teach me your way, LORD,
    that I may rely on your faithfulness;
give me an undivided heart,
    that I may fear your name.
I will praise you, Lord my God, with all my
heart;
    I will glorify your name forever.
For great is your love toward me.

PSALM 86:11-13